These Birds Can't Fly!

by Vita Richman

Scott Foresman
is an imprint of

Glenview, Illinois • Boston, Massachusetts • Mesa, Arizona
Shoreview, Minnesota • Upper Saddle River, New Jersey

Photographs

Every effort has been made to secure permission and provide appropriate credit for photographic material. The publisher deeply regrets any omission and pledges to correct errors called to its attention in subsequent editions.

Unless otherwise acknowledged, all photographs are the property of Pearson Education.

Photo locators denoted as follows: Top (T), Center (C), Bottom (B), Left (L), Right (R), Background (Bkgd)

Cover: ©Digital Vision; **1** ©Digital Stock; **3** (BL, CR) ©DK Images; **4** ©Digital Vision; **5** ©Digital Stock; **6** ©DK Images; **7** ©DK Images; **8** (TR) ©Digital Stock, (CL) ©Maron/Fotolia, (CR) ©DK Images; **9** (CL, TC) ©DK Images, (TR) ©Nina Leen/Time & Life Pictures/Getty Images; **10** ©DK Images; **11** ©Maron/Fotolia; **12** ©Gary Ombler/DK Images; **13** ©Nina Leen/Time & Life Pictures/Getty Images; **14** ©DK Images

ISBN 13: 978-0-328-39419-7
ISBN 10:   0-328-39419-X

7 8 9 10 V0FL 16 15 14 13

Many birds cannot fly! They are called flightless birds.

Flightless birds are different from flying birds. Their bones are heavier than those of flying birds. Flightless birds' feathers are different too.

Like humans, all birds have a sternum, or breastbone. A flightless bird's sternum is different from that of a flying bird since there are no flight muscles attached to it.

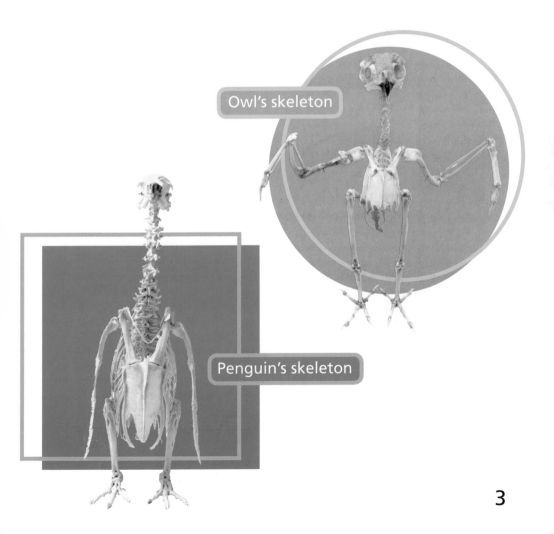

Owl's skeleton

Penguin's skeleton

Penguins are flightless birds that swim underwater. They have **flippers** instead of wings. Many penguins live on and around the **frozen** continent of Antarctica.

You may have seen penguins in an aquarium **cuddle** and **snuggle** with their chicks. Have you ever watched a penguin **preen**, or clean and smooth its feathers?

Penguin

Ostriches are the largest birds in the world. They live in Africa. Male ostriches can weigh three hundred pounds!

Ostriches eat plants. Female ostriches lay up to twelve eggs over a period of about three weeks. Both parents guard the nest while waiting for the eggs to **hatch**. An egg hatches when the chick inside **pecks** its way out of it.

Ostrich

Ostrich eggs

Emus live in Australia. They have shaggy, gray-brown feathers and long, powerful legs.

Emus eat fruit, seeds, plants, and insects. Female emus can lay up to ten bluish-green eggs at one time. Male emus sit on the nests for about fifty-five days, until the chicks hatch.

Emu

Cassowaries are found in the swamps and rain forests of Australia and New Guinea. They have bony helmets on their heads. They have sharp claws and three toes on each foot.

Cassowaries weigh about 130 pounds. They eat fruit, insects, frogs, and snakes.

Cassowary

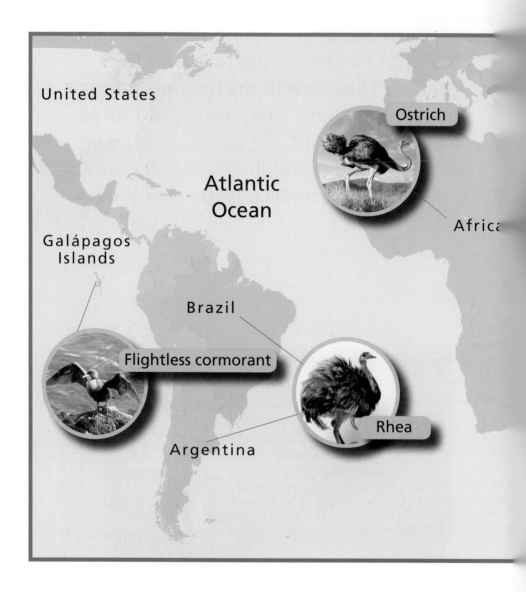

United States

Atlantic Ocean

Ostrich

Africa

Galápagos Islands

Brazil

Flightless cormorant

Rhea

Argentina

This world map shows the homes of many flightless birds. Do any of these birds live in the country where you live? Have you ever traveled to a country where flightless birds live?

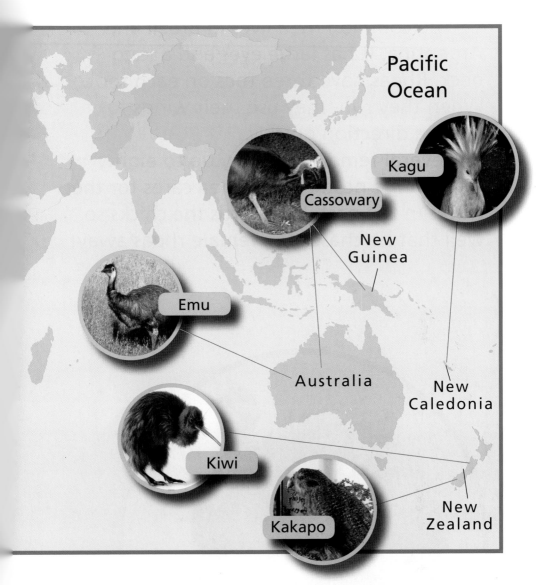

Pacific Ocean

Kagu

Cassowary

New Guinea

Emu

Australia

New Caledonia

Kiwi

Kakapo

New Zealand

Scientists believe that the ancestors of flightless birds could fly. Scientists also think that flightless birds became flightless because the animals that once hunted them became extinct.

The common rhea lives in Brazil and Argentina. It has large eyes and a long neck. Rheas have three toes on each foot. When they run, they use their wings to change direction quickly.

Several female rheas lay up to eighty eggs in one nest. A male rhea cares for the chicks in the nest. He guards the chicks so well that he chases the female rheas away!

Rhea

Flightless cormorants are rare. They are found only on the Galápagos Islands. They have few feathers and are black in color. They weigh about nine pounds.

Flightless cormorants have webbed feet and are great swimmers. When flightless cormorants come back to shore after a swim, they hold out their wings to dry.

Flightless cormorant

Kakapos are parrots found in New Zealand. They have shiny, yellow-green feathers. The feathers on their faces make them look like owls.

Kakapos live alone. When it is time to mate, male kakapos make a booming sound to attract females. The sound of male kakapos booming can be heard from more than four miles away.

Kakapo

Kagus live on the island of New Caledonia in the South Pacific Ocean. They are called "the ghosts of the forest" because of their pale gray feathers. They like to eat snails, worms, and lizards.

Kagus are endangered because of hunting by dogs and cats. And kagu parents raise only one chick a year.

Kagu

Have you ever eaten a kiwi fruit? There is a flightless bird called the kiwi. It lives in New Zealand. A kiwi is about the size of a chicken.

Kiwis have very long beaks with nostrils at the end. Their nostrils help them smell the insects and worms they like to eat. The kiwis' whiskers help them feel their way through tight spaces.

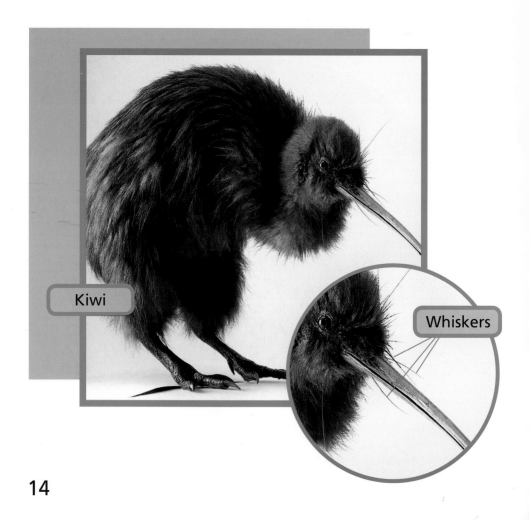

Kiwi

Whiskers

Wow! We have taken quite a tour of the world of flightless birds! From emus to kiwis to ostriches, you have now learned much about these unique creatures. Here are a few more interesting facts about flightless birds.

Flightless-Bird Facts

Ostrich fossils date back five million years.

There may be as many as 725,000 emus living today.

Kakapos are in danger of becoming extinct.

Cassowaries can live for more than sixty years.

Glossary

cuddle *v.* to lie closely and comfortably; curl up.

flippers *n.* broad, flat body parts used for swimming by animals such as seals and penguins.

frozen *adj.* hardened with cold; turned into ice.

hatch *v.* to bring forth young; open.

pecks *v.* strikes at with the beak.

preen *v.* to smooth or arrange the feathers with the beak.

snuggle *v.* to lie closely and comfortably together; nestle; cuddle.